Everything Is True at Once

Everything Is True at Once

BART GALLE

9/30/10
To Bonnie –
old CEE friends
–Bart Galle

PASSAGER BOOKS
Baltimore, MD
2010

FIRST EDITION
Published 2010 by Passager Books
ISBN: 978-0-9631385-7-6

COVER DESIGN: Pantea Amin Tofangchi

Passager Books is in residence at the University of Baltimore
in the School of Communications Design.

PASSAGER BOOKS
1420 North Charles Street
Baltimore, Maryland 21201
www.passagerpress.com

ACKNOWLEDGMENTS:
Grateful acknowledgment is made to the following publications,
in which these poems first appeared:
Coe Review: "What I Believe"
Minnetonka Review: "My Father's Hands, Like Birds Themselves," "On
Burning Old Maps," "When a Butterfly Ran into Me," "Your Painting
of an Iris, Unfinished"
r.kv.r.y: "Father's Day" (as "Postcards from the Dead"), "You Will Not
Find It Here" (as "The Meaning of Smiles")
Water-Stone Review: "Reading My Son's Autopsy Report"
White Pelican Review: "Batting Cages," "What Remains," "Playing Cars"

"At the Mirror," "Kingfisher" and "My Mother Decides to Remodel"
won the 2008 *Passager* Poetry Contest.
"What Remains" won the Fall 2009 Hollingsworth Prize for
an oustanding poem from *White Pelican Review.*

Funding provided in part by a grant from the Minnesota State Arts Board,
through an appropriation by the Minnesota State Legislature,
a grant from the National Endowment for the Arts and private funders.

Note:
The lines in italics at the end of "Father's Day" are from *Good Night
Moon* by Margaret Wise Brown.

Bart Sr and Alex by Bart Galle, soft pastel, 22x26, 2003

*To my wife, Lynn, our sons, David and Michael,
my mother, Dorothy, and the continuing presence
of my father, Bart Sr, and son, Alex*

Sometimes the way to milk and honey is through the body.
Sometimes the way is in a song.
But there are three ways in the world:
dangerous, wounding, and beauty.

LINDA HOGAN

Where is the center of the sea?
Why do waves never go there?

Why do the waves ask me
the same questions I ask them?

PABLO NERUDA

CONTENTS

BATTING CAGES

This is where ten-year-old boys
chew their gum and put on batting gloves
and grip the bats they had to have
and take the proper stance and dream
the hit, and where the hollow pipe sound
of bats on balls and the jingling
of chain-link fences and slamming
of cage doors are all good,
part of the business of sport, and where
things are taken to the next level,
and the laughter of boys erupts
when a swing is not even close
and again
because the batter is laughing, too,
has dropped his bat,
has fallen to his knees, laughing,

can't stand up.
And the balls go by.

And this is where, some nights,
despite the trophies, despite
the win, you didn't get a hit,
believe you will never get a hit
again,
so after the game,
you step into a cage,
and while you perfect
the art of missing,
I step into another
to watch
and wait for the ball
to hit me
in the heart
and the next ball
to hit me
in the heart,
one swing at a time.

READING MY SON'S AUTOPSY REPORT

Death is not found, just the fact of it.
Nor is the secret to what went wrong,
only that tragedy is largely unremarkable
and within normal limits. The chords of your heart

are delicate, your kindness to a child palpable.
Your liver and kidneys are smooth and glistening,
as if examined in moonlight and washed
in black, icy waters.

The bag you come in, the things you wear
and bring for the journey, your shorts,
undershirt, a gray metal watch,
two rings, metal hoop

earrings, a pack of cigarettes,
$25.05 in coins. Your posture of repose,
your reluctant awakening to the Y-shaped
thoracic incision. Forgive me

for entering your room and going through
your things. I wish the sad,
angry substance of you were here to yell
and push me speechless to the floor.

AT THE MIRROR

It's hard to brush your teeth and cry
at the same time:
the flagellation of the bristles

and the determination to be thorough
demand attention.
There's also something comic

about a tear-streaked face
and foaming mouth;
the grimace in the mirror looks like

a mime's exaggerated
anguish, as if you
were only practicing grief.

YOU WILL NOT FIND IT HERE

1
We went to the Chuck Close exhibit at MoMA.
Pores the size of a thumb. Hairs like wire.

I still like Norman Rockwell, you said.
You respected his craftsmanship and his eye

for human nature. Your rendition of
"The Artist's Dilemma" was one of your best.

As we went through the galleries, girls
followed, until every girl in the museum

was in one room. You should be a model,
they told you in the coffee shop on 42nd Street.

2

All the mirrors have been torn out
or covered by cardboard
gouged with ball-point self-caricatures
reminiscent of Francis Bacon
and messages to yourself like
"Don't Pick" or "Prozac Is Your Friend."

3

Let me hold your face.
Let me be your mirror.

4

The walls of your room are scarred
by martial-arts throwing-stars
and there is a hole made by a fist.

In a drawer are loose keys, a picture
of your girlfriend, some baseball medals,
an envelope with a phone number on it,

and a folder of pictures you have drawn.
At the top of one a hand reaches down
with a corkscrew

that goes through a head
being lifted off a figure
in a shirt and tie. Hands reach up

to retrieve what is being lost.
The corkscrew is long and looks like
the rope of a noose.

"The Friendly Hand of Depression,"
like all your drawings,
is rendered in meticulous detail.

Particular attention has been paid
to the wrinkles in the shirt
and the pattern in the tie.

5
I am looking at photographs.
I pull one out
from our trip to New York.

You are leaning against the balustrade
in Brooklyn Heights, Manhattan
in the background, the web
of the Brooklyn Bridge to the right.

You are wearing a cap, visor
tightly curled, and a polo shirt.
You are smiling.

I look at the smile,
and try to trace it back to something
I can trust – perhaps the picture we chose
for your obituary:

you are helping two young girls
with an art project. Or the double portrait
of you and a dog. Or the picture of you
between your grandparents,

the summer you stayed with them up north
and built my father a bench
so he could rest beside the road.

If those three smiles are a word
and it means *happy*,
one might think the language is easy,

but there is a smile
that can be called *appears to be happy*,
one that can be *showing happiness*,
and another *wanting to make happy*
and even *concealing pain*.

It is like facing a Chuck Close portrait,
focusing on a single square
filled with a whorl of paint
whose tip might signify
the upturned curve of a smile
or a glint of light
or a brushstroke coming to an end,

and realizing that next to it
there is another square, almost the same,
and another above it,
and that whatever it is you are looking for,
you will not find it here.

YOUR PAINTING OF AN IRIS, UNFINISHED

I'd like to say the blossom is there
without the supporting structure;
that, typical of youth,
there was a rush to fulfillment,
followed by a loss of interest.
But no.
The leaves and stems are complete
and carefully rendered
in icy blue-greens
and mottled ochres. A bud
is finished, as is a lesser flower
in the lower right
designed to balance
the full one in the upper left.
That's the one left undone.
The outer petals are finished,
some in a saturated purple,

others in a pale blue wash,
but the heart of it is blank,

just penciled in, a gaping hole
right where our eyes
are forced to go.

FIRST DREAM

Imagine embracing someone you love,
being embraced.

That was the dream.

> They say that newborn giraffes
> fall six feet to start breathing.

When I hit the ground,
I still felt the smooth warmth of your shoulders.
Then you cooled into death again.

I was alone in a hotel room in Las Vegas,

> breathing.

SOMETIMES MOVEMENT

Crossing campus, thinking large ideas
of how the earth lays down its history
or the body suddenly sickens:

on the mall a small commotion in a bush –
a common sparrow tangled
in some unspooled audiotape and string.

I approach as death might, and a close heart
beats percussive wings.
       An exchange is made:
             I give it freedom.
             It takes freedom back.

Sometimes we see the movement
of a single leaf
           where the wind begins.

Sometimes the world just opens to a page,
and we remember
           our first lessons.

THE HAND THAT MATTERS

Imagine the young apprentice
painting the Pope's hand
while Titian sits in the corner,
waiting to finish the background.
Sometimes it's not the hand that matters,
even if it wears a sacred ring,
but the just-right color
of the surrounding space
that confers a holy aura
to a graying beard and wrinkled robe.
It's not the hand that holds the purse,
but those ships in the harbor that fill it with gold
or the dots of distant foliage that echo
the pearls on the mistress' neck.

Of course, the picture my grandson drew of me
had no background.
He saw no need for that or even

for a body. My fingers
grew directly from my head, like hairs.

If there were a you like that,
I'd lace my fingers into yours,
hold you close –
there'd be no far – no day
or night, no summer
losing its warmth to fall,
no place
for a face
I loved so well
to suddenly
disappear.

EVERYTHING IS TRUE AT ONCE

1

I reach to nudge the visor on my cap,
but it's lying on the couch,
where I left it when I took my nap.

My head still feels its firm embrace,
while on the dance floor of my brain
                           a song plays
that I listened to when I was twelve
and thought I was in love.

            Time is generous in many ways.

I don't know if the man who
                           sang that song
is alive or dead,
but I'll be generous, too:

he's alive, and he's still singing.

2
I smell the plaster drying on the wall,
so tomorrow I can sand and paint.
I'll finally have that fist hole covered over.
But that's enough for closure.
I'm more of a believer in

　　　everything is true at once.

The autumn sun has moved across my desk
and just fell off the edge.
Some warmth remains, which I'm collecting
with my palm –
　　　heat going up
　　　as night comes down

in this unfinished world.

FATHER'S DAY

1
Our grief group meets in a room
where children draw turkeys
by tracing around their hands;
where children hang strips of purple ribbon
as reminders of the homeless.

We are homeless, too,
and trace outlines of our stories
over and over, wishing
we had a simple word for them,
like *hand.*

2
At first, caught in the torrent
of our individual loss, we barely hear. Slowly
we become generous with our grief, and one death
becomes many. Not the many of Treblinka

or Cambodia or Darfur, where
many is a particle of dust. Not even

the many of Omaha Beach, where you
can walk among the crosses and Stars
of David or read names and see
to the end of the white rows that fit
beneath the trees, or huddle with the German dead
distant from the beach, face-to-face
under squat black crosses.
This is the many of

Josh, Georgie, Alex, Sarah, Tank, DaJuan,
Elizabeth, Megan, William.

3
The stages of grief have left for the day.

A man wanted to move on, so he sold his house. Now
he lives in two houses.

Grief flows to the sea where everything is true at once,
every story matters.

> *Coyote wanted people to die because they*
> *had fingers and he only had paws.*

Tell us more stories, but be specific.
Name names.

4
We bring our dead with us when we meet.
They gather in the corner, all of them
young: the one who fell from a cliff, the one who

accidentally shot himself, the two who died
of a drug overdose, the three who were hit by a car.
They play with the child who fell

from a window. When they hear their names,
they look up and listen to us talk about replaying

a message on an answering machine,

smelling an unwashed shirt,
seeing initials and a birth date on a license plate.
We see them

in a college student waiting for a bus,
a toddler carried from a car to daycare, a boy
shooting baskets before supper.

When laughter erupts at a restaurant table,
I turn to look for you. When leaves rattle
in the poplar grove, I enter and look for you.

If only the living knew such love.

5
Then one day they are gone.
They don't need us anymore.

6

The woman in the picture looks at me, her grin
almost a grimace. She is reclining
on the grass, arms back, legs drawn up.

She wears jeans and a tank top,
probably a public yard worker on break,
her bamboo rake off to the side.

She is Latina, full-bodied,
and looks as if she could carry me
like a sack of groceries.

She stares at me from a photograph
I bought at an art fair
and hung over my computer at work.

I look to her for joy,
but occasionally
she mocks me, puts me in my place,

as my son would sometimes do.
I imagine her laughing for him
waiting to meet him at the end of her shift –

say, in the square in San Miguel on Cozumel –
handing him her rake to carry,
him refusing, as he would; them sparring

on the way to a little restaurant,
where perhaps the others who are dead
sit at a table with their drinks,

including two for them. Because
if we don't get postcards from the dead,
we send them to ourselves.

7
I keep a Father's Day card from you
on my desk.
It has a picture of a moon on it.

You wrote that it reminded you of days
before depression and drugs,
when I would read you bedtime stories from a book

that had a moon on its cover.
Good night moon.
Good night cow jumping over the moon.

Good night stars.
Good night air.
Good night noises everywhere.

It was a card you sent yourself
from the dead. I open the card,
look at the words, the letters,

the lines, then imagine the pencil,
then the hand, the arm, the head bent over,
concentrating, moving the hand.

watercolor, 13x13, 1999

Unfinished Iris (Alex) "Your Painting of an Iris, Unfinished" watercolor, 9x12, 2000

Formation of Geese (Bart Galle Sr) "A Bird Worth Shooting" watercolor, 14x12, 1968

Slippers by the Shed Door (Bart) "What Remains" soft pastel, 17x17, 2003

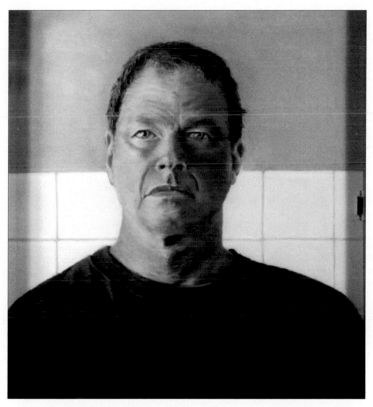

At the Mirror (Bart) "At the Mirror" soft pastel, 22x24, 2006

Artist's Dilemma (after Norman Rockwell) (Alex)
"You Will Not Find It Here" watercolor, 9x12, 1998

The Friendly Hand of Depression (Alex)
"You Will Not Find It Here" colored pencil, 8x11, 2000

Forgotten Lures (Bart) "What Remains" soft pastel, 12x15, 2003

MY FATHER'S HANDS, LIKE BIRDS THEMSELVES

When I was twelve I helped my father
clean grouse in the garage

on a piece of plywood
set across two sawhorses.

With a hatchet he chopped off
heads, feet, and wings,

then tore off feathers,
and threw it all in a bucket.

Cradling a body, he slit it open
to the liver, the gizzard, the limp intestinal string,

and the rasp of his thumbnail
on the fretwork of the ribs.

He handed me the little clot of a heart
and guided my fingers on the mysterious crop,

kneading the bumps of juniper berries
and grit of roadside gravel picked up the night before.

My hands were numb and red up to the wrists
in a galvanized tub of icy water,

my father's hands like birds themselves.

WHAT REMAINS

One night, while fishing from the dock,
my father stuck a spinner and a buck tail jig
into the bark of a cedar tree.

When he died, they were still there,
and when the tree came down, they were there.
I cut away the square of bark that held the hooks

so I could make a shadow box:
restore the luster of the yellow beads,
steel-wool some rust away, bleach the strands

of buck tail that remained. Instead
I left the lures the way they were and nailed the bark
onto the shed, above the sturdy door my father made

to keep out bear. When it bangs against the jamb,
the spinner shakes and, sometimes, flashes,
the silver flecks still there.

A BIRD WORTH SHOOTING

You always said that any tie
with a pheasant or a duck on it
was a tie you'd gladly wear.
So when you started painting
in your fifties,
coming home from work
and spreading out your watercolors
on your workbench,
it was only natural that your subjects
would be game birds.

Your painting of geese in formation
was one of your favorites —
the steel gray sky, the geese rising in a V
from the bottom right,
the challenge of painting something
you knew and cared about,
something you loved enough
to shoot

and drag from the ice-stiffened marsh,
then clean and cook for dinner.

I'm looking at a particular goose.
The black expanse of the left wing,
feathers adjusting to the wind.
The far wing foreshortened
and slightly torqued.
The loaf of the breast glowing
like golden wheat.

Father, let me praise your work.
I've seen that bird before.
I've seen you raise a gun to it.

ON BURNING OLD MAPS

I could say it's because
I finally know my way or
the world has changed again,
but really it's about
coffee stains, campfire soot,
scribbled notes – *I took the canoe*,
streams that change their course
because they're torn and taped,
the accumulated burden
of abandoned plans.
It's about a map drawer
that won't close.

The hands that strike the match
look like my father's hands.
They have the same topography
and markings, as familiar
as the trail to the beaver pond
or the path along the ridge

past the new-growth pine
and columbine. As the fire
burns down, I imagine
the rocky climb
to the campsite on the palisade
and the view of the lake below,
black and ringed with trees,
like an open drawer
with a star in it.

A BIRD'S LIFE

Our cockatiel is eating the piano
nip by nip. One day we'll come home
to just a twisted jawbone
of keys and sprung bouquet of wires.
Or, like sorrow overtaking joy,
the bird will swallow the piano whole,
and a feathered baby grand
will hover near the ceiling,
moving on small wings
between the living room
and dining room, until
the cockatiel becomes herself again,
and life returns to normal.

It is spring.
My wife and I are raking the leaves
we should have raked last fall.
The cockatiel is shedding feathers.
We've hired some workers to paint

the upstairs. One of them is wearing
a wife-beater T-shirt like our son wore.
When the bird lands on his shoulder
and starts to sing – her dead master
has returned – he tips a can of paint,
which bleeds across the floor.

The vet says her chewing
represents nesting behavior.
He thinks she is adjusting well
and will outlive us all.
Now she has discovered
our Southwestern pottery collection
and a favorite oil: the half-mortal,
half-spirit Nanabozho as a child,
sleeping in the arms of Nokomis.

MY FATHER'S WORKBENCH

The first time we grieve, it seems
forever. We think our sorrow will run out, but
     it never does.

Which brings me to your workbench
and this box of carpenter's crayons with
     just one missing

and this tray of single-edged razor
blades, each one wrapped in its own
     protective sleeve.

I used a blade the other day to shape
a piece of molding. It slid into place
     with a snap.

And I shaved the broken ends of a bass rod
so I could join them together, rather than
     buy a new one.

I tried to use the crayons. They held such promise,
yellow and hexagonal,
     like a beehive,

but they were blunt and imprecise.
I kept looking for a pencil. So I gave them
     to the children.

That was why you bought in bulk,
often beyond all reason – your faith
     in the future.

I'm not sure that I share your faith,
but I love the naked beauty
     of each new blade

laid open in its wrapper
and the way the wood grips the blade,
     pulling it deep

into the wound. I love the way
they help me fit my life together
and sharpen

my intentions to a fine point,
leaving nothing but the shavings'
breaking waves.

MY MOTHER DECIDES TO REMODEL

Tired of her aging walls,
my mother decides to paint them.
She paints her bedroom delft blue,
the kitchen apricot. She maneuvers
around the hospital bed
where my father died
to paint the guest room cerise.
To clear a path to heaven,
she paints the ceilings transcendent white.
The living room and dining room are
Sea Mist Green and Nantucket Green.
The time spent choosing has earned
them proper names, which she recites
as if they are new relatives or boarders
she has taken in. My mother
has a new glow now when she sits
at her kitchen table drinking a cup of coffee,
an apricot glow, in fact,
and she is quick to give tours

of her rainbow rooms that say,
This was inside me, and there's more.
There's always a stop to kneel and feel
the plush nap of her finishing touch,
the Ottoman rugs, deep pools of burgundy
and green. *They cost a little bit more*, she says,
*but even with the paint, the whole thing
was cheaper than a coffin.*

PLAYING CARS

for my grandsons

It starts as it should, with roads
and intersections and stop signs
and refueling, but then somehow
we're flying and the whole room
is in play, and the demolition starts,
and cars are crashing everywhere,
on chairs and sofas,
and falling from the sky
into shark-infested seas,
and a science is devised
for knuckle protection,
and, finally, when the carpet
is a graveyard of tiny
silver chasses, we slump our way
from war to pleasure, as every
epic must, and I run a car
up and down his back
until he shivers,

and then I try another,
and he hands me one to try
and then another, and we test
the wheels of joy until
my arms go numb.

KINGFISHER

At the end of a dock
a young boy kneels,
his grandfather
sits on a tackle box.
They study a worm
with its own ideas
about hooks
and the form
of things to come.
In the water below,
blue gills hover
in the cover of the shade.
A bay away
two eagles teach
their young to
plummet for prey,
while a kingfisher
does what works for him
by whipping a frog

against a tree
in time-honored
kingfisher fashion.
Soon the rattle
of its call,
then the stitches
of its flight
up and down the shore,
as a hook drops,
sunfish rise, and eagles
spread wet wings,
scattering sunlight
everywhere.

WHAT I BELIEVE

Airplanes should tear the sky as they pass through,
great folds of blue flopping to earth,
not pretend that flying is an easy thing –
as we leave signs of our relationship
so as not to wander off
in our ant-like comings and goings.

I saw your note on the counter –
at the store. I pictured you
turning a peach on its cushion of fuzz,
holding it to your nose to test its heavy scent.

I don't believe the world's a round and spinning thing.
The water in the children's pool sloshes
only when they play in it. Groceries don't tumble
from the bags as we carry them to the house.
When you come home, I won't float away
into the trees before I kiss you.

WHEN A BUTTERFLY RAN INTO ME

I knew the wind
had bones. And intent.
And sometimes
drank too much.
Which made for
an interesting tale
if one could
follow its flight.
Orange hawkweed.
Pearly everlasting.
Moss-covered boulder
in a collar of horse hair
fern. Crooked birch
ready to fall
at the foot of a dock
slapped by waves
dragged down the lake
by muscular clouds.
Darkening sky.

And aging human
sitting in a chair,
stubbornly planted
right in the middle
of everything.

IN LEGENDS, the crane stands for longevity, peace, harmony, good fortune and fidelity. A high flyer, it is cherished for its ability to see both heaven and earth. These ancient, magnificent birds, so crucial in the wild as an "umbrella species," are now endangered and must be protected.

Passager Books is dedicated to making public the passions of a generation vital to our survival. We invite you to help us carry out our mission.

Everything Is True at Once was designed by Pantea Amin Tofangchi. The text pages are set in Adobe Garamond Pro, the text paper is vanilla Finch opaque vellum. Printed in an edition of 250 by BookMobile in Minneapolis, Minnesota.

The editors are delighted to present *Everything Is True at Once* by Bart Galle, the third in a series of chapbooks: *Six over Sixty*, by writers whose work has appeared in *Passager*. These limited-edition chapbooks will be available individually and as a set.

ALSO FROM PASSAGER BOOKS

A Cartography of Peace
by Jean L. Connor

Improvise in the Amen Corner
by Larnell Custis Butler

A Little Breast Music
by Shirley J. Brewer

A Hinge of Joy
by Jean L. Connor

Keeping Time
150 Years of Journal Writing
Edited by Mary Azrael & Kendra Kopelke